In Mad Love
and War

Also by Joy Harjo

Joy Harjo

In Mad Love and War

Wesleyan University Press
Middletown, Connecticut

Published by Wesleyan University Press
Middletown, CT 06459
www.wesleyan.edu/wespress

Printed in the United States of America
15 14 13 12

ISBN for the paperback edition: 978-0-8195-1182-9

Some of the poems in this book appeared originally in
*The Anthology of Contemporary Arizona Indian Litera-
ture, Bloomsbury Review, Calapooya Collage, Condi-
tions, Contact II, Continental Drifter, Early Ripening,
Fish Drum, Harper's Anthology of Twentieth-Century
Native American Poetry, Journal of Ethnic Studies, Mas-
sachusetts Review, Nimrod, Ploughshares, Rhetorical
Review, River Styx,* and *Tyuonyi.* "For Anna Mae Pictou
Aquash" originally appeared in *And the Ground Spoke*
(Guadalupe Cultural Arts Center, 1986).

The excerpt from "Grand Army Plaza," by June Jordan,
from *Passion* (copyright © 1980 by June Jordan), is re-
printed by permission of Beacon Press. The excerpt from
"Lucille," by Kenny Rogers, is reprinted by permission of
SBK Entertainment World. The title "Strange Fruit" is re-
printed by permission of Edward B. Marks.

Artwork courtesy of Jaune Quick-to-See Smith.

Library of Congress Cataloging-in-Publication Data
Harjo, Joy.
   In mad love and war / Joy Harjo.—1st ed.
      p.   cm.
   ISBN 0-8195-2180-9.—ISBN 0-8195-1182-X (pbk.)
   I. Title.
PS3558.A6242316   1990
811'.54—dc20   89-34102

For my children, Phil Dayn and Rainy Dawn
For Laura Newman
And the music

I wish to acknowledge Leslie from the very beginning, for her loving encouragement. You helped me understand the importance of story, and my place in it, and were always there, whether it was with new gossip, a typewriter, or your relentless vision. I wish also to thank Audre for her warrior self, her fierce and tender poetry. You helped me affirm that the erotic belongs in poetry, as in the self. There is no separation. And finally my thanks to Brenda, who once again, as with horses, played the magic arranger with mad love.

I appreciate your love.

Contents

In Mad Love and War

Grace

I think of Wind and her wild ways the year we had nothing to lose
and lost it anyway in the cursed country of the fox. We still talk
about that winter, how the cold froze imaginary buffalo on the stuffed
horizon of snowbanks. The haunting voices of the starved and mutilated
broke fences, crashed our thermostat dreams, and we couldn't stand it
one more time. So once again we lost a winter in stubborn memory, walked
through cheap apartment walls, skated through fields of ghosts into
a town that never wanted us, in the epic search for grace.

Like Coyote, like Rabbit, we could not contain our terror and clowned
our way through a season of false midnights. We had to swallow
that town with laughter, so it would go down easy as honey. And one
morning as the sun struggled to break ice, and our dreams had found us
with coffee and pancakes in a truck stop along Highway 80,
we found grace.

I could say grace was a woman with time on her hands, or a white
buffalo escaped from memory. But in that dingy light it was a promise
of balance. We once again understood the talk of animals, and spring
was lean and hungry with the hope of children and corn.

I would like to say, with grace, we picked ourselves up and walked
into the spring thaw. We didn't; the next season was worse. You went
home to Leech Lake to work with the tribe and I went south. And, Wind,
I am still crazy. I know there is something larger than the memory
of a dispossessed people. We have seen it.

(For Wind and Jim Welch)

1

The Wars

We are not survivors of a civil war

We survive our love
because we go on

loving

    —June Jordan
        from "Grand Army Plaza"

Deer Dancer

Nearly everyone had left that bar in the middle of winter except the hardcore. It was the coldest night of the year, every place shut down, but not us. Of course we noticed when she came in. We were Indian ruins. She was the end of beauty. No one knew her, the stranger whose tribe we recognized, her family related to deer, if that's who she was, a people accustomed to hearing songs in pine trees, and making them hearts.

The woman inside the woman who was to dance naked in the bar of misfits blew deer magic. Henry Jack, who could not survive a sober day, thought she was Buffalo Calf Woman come back, passed out, his head by the toilet. All night he dreamed a dream he could not say. The next day he borrowed money, went home, and sent back the money I lent. Now that's a miracle. Some people see vision in a burned tortilla, some in the face of a woman.

This is the bar of broken survivors, the club of shotgun, knife wound, of poison by culture. We who were taught not to stare drank our beer. The players gossiped down their cues. Someone put a quarter in the jukebox to relive despair. Richard's wife dove to kill her. We had to hold her back, empty her pockets of knives and diaper pins, buy her two beers to keep her still, while Richard secretly bought the beauty a drink.

How do I say it? In this language there are no words for how the real world collapses. I could say it in my own and the sacred mounds would come into focus, but I couldn't take it in this dingy envelope. So I look at the stars in this strange city, frozen to the back of the sky, the only promises that ever make sense.

My brother-in-law hung out with white people, went to law school with a perfect record, quit. Says you can keep your laws, your words. And practiced law on the street with his hands. He jimmied to the proverbial dream girl, the face of the moon, while the players racked a new game. He bragged to us, he told her magic words and that's when she broke, became human.
But we all heard his bar voice crack:

What's a girl like you doing in a place like this?

That's what I'd like to know, what are we all doing in a place like this?

You would know she could hear only what she wanted to; don't we all? Left the drink of betrayal Richard bought her, at the bar. What was she on? We all wanted some. Put a quarter in the juke. We all take risks stepping into thin air. Our ceremonies didn't predict this. Or we expected more.

I had to tell you this, for the baby inside the girl sealed up with a lick of hope and swimming into praise of nations. This is not a rooming house, but a dream of winter falls and the deer who portrayed the relatives of strangers. The way back is deer breath on icy windows.

The next dance none of us predicted. She borrowed a chair for the stairway to heaven and stood on a table of names. And danced in the room of children without shoes.

You picked a fine time to leave me, Lucille.
With four hungry children and a crop in the field.

And then she took off her clothes. She shook loose memory, waltzed with the empty lover we'd all become.

She was the myth slipped down through dreamtime. The promise of feast we all knew was coming. The deer who crossed through knots of a curse to find us. She was no slouch, and neither were we, watching.

The music ended. And so does the story. I wasn't there. But I imagined her like this, not a stained red dress with tape on her heels but the deer who entered our dream in white dawn, breathed mist into pine trees, her fawn a blessing of meat, the ancestors who never left.

For Anna Mae Pictou Aquash, Whose Spirit Is Present
Here and in the Dappled Stars (for we remember the story
and must tell it again so we may all live)

Beneath a sky blurred with mist and wind,
                              I am amazed as I watch the violet
heads of crocuses erupt from the stiff earth
                              after dying for a season,
as I have watched my own dark head
                              appear each morning after entering
the next world
              to come back to this one,
                              amazed.
It is the way in the natural world to understand the place
                              the ghost dancers named
after the heart/breaking destruction.
                        Anna Mae,
                              everything and nothing changes.
You are the shimmering young woman
                        who found her voice,
when you were warned to be silent, or have your body cut away
from you like an elegant weed.
                  You are the one whose spirit is present in the dappled stars.
(They prance and lope like colored horses who stay with us
              through the streets of these steely cities. And I have seen them
                  nuzzling the frozen bodies of tattered drunks
                              on the corner.)
This morning when the last star is dimming
                        and the buses grind toward
the middle of the city, I know it is ten years since they buried you

In February 1976, an unidentified body of a young woman was found on the Pine Ridge Reserva-
tion in South Dakota. The official autopsy attributed death to exposure. The FBI agent present at
the autopsy ordered her hands severed and sent to Washington for fingerprinting. John Trudell
rightly called this mutilation an act of war. Her unnamed body was buried. When Anna Mae
Aquash, a young Micmac woman who was an active American Indian Movement member, was
discovered missing by her friends and relatives, a second autopsy was demanded. It was then
discovered she had been killed by a bullet fired at close range to the back of her head. Her killer
or killers have yet to be identified.

the second time in Lakota, a language that could

free you.

I heard about it in Oklahoma, or New Mexico,

how the wind howled and pulled everything down

in a righteous anger.

(It was the women who told me) and we understood wordlessly

the ripe meaning of your murder.

As I understand ten years later after the slow changing

of the seasons

that we have just begun to touch

the dazzling whirlwind of our anger,

we have just begun to perceive the amazed world the ghost dancers

entered

crazily, beautifully.

We Must Call a Meeting

I am fragile, a piece of pottery smoked from fire
                                        made of dung,
the design drawn from nightmares. I am an arrow, painted
                                            with lightning
to seek the way to the name of the enemy,
                                but the arrow has now created
its own language.
                    It is a language of lizards and storms, and we have
begun to hold conversations
                        long into the night.
                                            I forget to eat.
I don't work. My children are hungry and the animals who live
in the backyard are starving.
                            I begin to draw maps of stars.
The spirits of old and new ancestors perch on my shoulders.
I make prayers of clear stone
                        of feathers from birds
                                    who live closest to the gods.
The voice of the stone is born
                        of a meeting of yellow birds
who circle the ashes of a smoldering volcano.
                                The feathers sweep the prayers up
and away.
                I, too, try to fly but get caught in the cross fire of signals
                            and my spirit drops back down to earth.
I am lost; I am looking for you
                who can help me walk this thin line between the breathing
                                    and the dead.
You are the curled serpent in the pottery of nightmares.
You are the dreaming animal who paces back and forth in my head.
We must call a meeting.
                    Give me back my language and build a house

Inside it.

      A house of madness.

            A house for the dead who are not dead.

And the spiral of the sky above it.

And the sun

      and the moon.

           And the stars to guide us called promise.

Strange Fruit

I was out in the early evening, taking a walk in the fields to think about this poem I was writing, or walking to the store for a pack of cigarettes, a pound of bacon. How quickly I smelled evil, then saw the hooded sheets ride up in the not yet darkness, in the dusk carrying the moon, in the dust behind my tracks. Last night there were crosses burning in my dreams, and the day before a black cat stood in the middle of the road with a ghost riding its back. Something knocked on the window at midnight. My lover told me:

Shush, we have too many stories to carry on our backs like houses, we have struggled too long to let the monsters steal our sleep, sleep, go to sleep.

But I never woke up. Dogs have been nipping at my heels since I learned to walk. I was taught to not dance for a rotten supper on the plates of my enemies. My mother taught me well.

I have not been unkind to the dead, nor have I been stingy with the living. I have not been with anyone else's husband, or anyone else's wife. I need a song. I need a cigarette. I want to squeeze my baby's legs, see her turn into a woman just like me. I want to dance under the full moon, or in the early morning on my lover's lap.

See this scar under my arm. It's from tripping over a rope when I was small; I was always a little clumsy. And my long, lean feet like my mother's have known where to take me, to where the sweet things grow. Some grow on trees, and some grow in other places.

But not this tree.

I didn't do anything wrong. I did not steal from your mother. My brother did not take your wife. I did not break into your home, tell you how to live or die. Please. Go away, hooded ghosts from hell on earth. I only want heaven

The title is from a song by Lewis Allan, often sung by Billie Holiday.

in my baby's arms, my baby's arms. Down the road through the trees I see the kitchen light on and my lover fixing supper, the baby fussing for her milk, waiting for me to come home. The moon hangs from the sky like a swollen fruit.

My feet betray me, dance anyway from this killing tree.

(For Jacqueline Peters, a vital writer, activist in her early thirties, who was lynched in Lafayette, California, in June 1986. She had been working to start a local NAACP chapter, in response to the lynching of a twenty-three-year-old black man, Timothy Lee, in November 1985, when she was hanged in an olive tree by the Ku Klux Klan.)

Trickster

Crow, in the new snow.
You caw, caw
    like crazy.
Laugh.
Because you know I'm a fool
too, like you
skimming over the thin ice
to the war going on
all over the world.

Autobiography

We lived next door to the bootlegger, and were lucky. The bootlegger reigned. We were a stolen people in a stolen land. Oklahoma meant defeat. But the sacred lands have their own plans, seep through fingers of the alcohol spirit. Nothing can be forgotten, only left behind.

Last week I saw the river where the hickory stood; this homeland doesn't predict a legacy of malls and hotels. Dreams aren't glass and steel but made from the hearts of deer, the blazing eye of a circling panther. Translating them was to understand the death count from Alabama, the destruction of grandchildren, famine of stories. I didn't think I could stand it. My father couldn't. He searched out his death with the vengeance of a warrior who has been the hunted. It's in our blood.

Even at two I knew we were different. Could see through the eyes of strangers that we were trespassers in the promised land. The Sooner State glorified the thief. Everyone and no one was Indian. You'd best forget, claim a white star. At three my mother told me this story:

God decided to make people. He put the first batch in the oven, kept them in too long. They burned. These were the black people. God put in the next batch. They were uncooked, not done. These were the white people. But the next batch he cooked just right, and these were the Indian people, just like you.

By then I was confused.
At five I was designated to string beads in kindergarten. At seven I knew how to play chicken and win. And at fourteen I was drinking.

I found myself in a city in the Southwest at twenty-one, when my past came into focus. It was near midnight. We were walking home and there he was, curled in the snow on the sidewalk, that man from Jemez. We had all been cheated. He hid his shame beneath a cold, downy blanket. We hid ours in poems. We took him home, where he shivered and cried through the night like a fighting storm, then woke in the morning, knowing nothing. Later I would see him on the street, the same age I am now. It was my long dark hair that cued his daughter, the chili, the songs. And I talked to him as if he were my father, with that respect, that hunger.

I have since outlived that man from Jemez, my father and that ragged self I chased through precarious years. But I carry them with me the same as this body carries the heart as a drum. Yesterday there was rain traveling east to home. A hummingbird spoke. She was a shining piece of invisible memory, inside the raw cortex of songs. I knew then this was the Muscogee season of forgiveness, time of new corn, the spiraling dance.

Fury of Rain

Thunder beings dance the flooding streets
of this city, stripped naked to their electric skeletons.
I stand inside their wild and sacred ritual
on these streets of greasy rainbows
and see my own furious longing
erupt from the broken mask of change
to stone, to bear, to lightning.
Gut memory shakes this earth like a rattle,
knocking my teeth with heroic thunder.
I could have lied
and not seen my own death
dancing in the streets, the main shady
character forcing me to live.
What can I do but celebrate after
guarding the wreck for thirty-five years, in
this ceremony larger than a damp, suspicious city?
We are all in the belly of a laughing god
swimming the heavens, in this whirling circle.
What we haven't imagined will one day
spit us out
magnificent and simple.

Resurrection

Estelí
       this mountain town means something
               like the glass of bloody stars.
Your Spanish tongue will not be silent.
                  In my volcano heart
soldiers pace, watch over what they fear.
             One pretty one leans against his girlfriend.
They make promises, touch, plan to meet somewhere else
                    in this war.
Not far down the fevered street
           a trace of calypso
               laughter from a cantina.
We are all in a balloon that's about to split.
             Candles make oblique circles
in the barrio church, line the walls with prayers.
                 An aboriginal woman
as old as Momotombo fingers obsidian,
             recalls dreams, waits for the light
to begin to break. I don't imagine anything.
             Lizards chase themselves all night
over the tin roof of the motel.
          I rock in a barrage of fever
feel the breathing sweat of the whole town stop, pause
                and begin again.
I have no damned words to make violence fit neatly
               like wrapped packages
of meat to contain us safely.
          The songs here speak tenderly of honor and love
sweet melody is the undercurrent of gunfire
              yet
the wounded and the dead call out in words that sting
           like bitter limes.
(Ask the women who have given away the clothes of their dead children.

Estelí is a mountain town in Nicaragua, not far from the Honduran border.

Ask the frozen soul of a man who was found in the hole left
by his missing penis.)

They are talking, yet
                    the night could change.
We all watch for fire
                    for all the fallen dead to return
and teach us a language so terrible
                    it could resurrect us all.

Legacy

In Wheeling, West Virginia, inmates riot.
Two cut out the heart of a child rapist
and hold it steaming in a guard's face
because he will live
                                    to tell the story.
They know they have already died
of unrequited love
                                    and in another version
won't recognize the murdered
as he walks toward them
                                    disguised as the betrayed lover.
I don't know the ending,
or how this will make the bruised and broken
child live easier into the night
                                    of a split world,
where in one camp the destroyers
                                    have cooked up
a stench of past and maggots.
                                    And in the other
love begins a dance, a giveaway to honor
the destroyed with new names.
I don't know the ending.
But I know the legacy of maggots is wings.
And I understand how lovers can destroy everything
                                    together.

Mercy

Mercy
on this morning where in the air is a flash
of what could be the salvation of spring.

After all this winter,
I mean, it wasn't just devil snow that rode us hard.
Mail me to Jamaica.

I want to lie out on steaming beaches.
Find my way back through glacier ice another way.
Forget the massacres, proclamations of war,

rumors of wars.
I won't pour rifle shot through the guts of someone
I'm told is my enemy.

Hell, my own enemy is right here.
Can you look inside, see past the teeth worn down
by meat and anger,

can you see?

Sometimes the only filter
is a dead cat in the road.

Sucks your belly up to your teeth
in fear of what might happen to you; all your sins
chase you in the street,

string what you thought was the only you
into a greasy field. I want to enter the next world
filled with food, wine

and the finest fishing.
Safe, so safe, like a beach in Jamaica

where bloodstains have already
soaked through to the bottom of the Caribbean
so you don't have to see

unless this light
becomes a bayonet of sound, hands of fire
to lead you to yourself

until you cry

mercy.

Bird

The moon plays horn, leaning on the shoulder of the dark universe
to the infinite glitter of chance. Tonight I watched Bird kill himself,

larger than real life. I've always had a theory that some of us
are born with nerve endings longer than our bodies. Out to here,

farther than his convoluted scales could reach. Those nights he
played did he climb the stairway of forgetfulness, with his horn,

a woman who is always beautiful to strangers? All poets
understand the final uselessness of words. We are chords to

other chords to other chords, if we're lucky, to melody. The moon
is brighter than anything I can see when I come out of the theater,

than music, than memory of music, or any mere poem. At least
I can dance to "Ornithology" or sweet-talk beside "Charlie's Blues,"

but inside this poem I can't play a horn, hijack a plane to
somewhere where music is the place those nerve endings dangle.

Each rhapsody embodies counterpoint, and pain stuns the woman
in high heels, the man behind the horn, beats the heart.

To survive is sometimes a leap into madness. The fingers of
saints are still hot from miracles, but can they save themselves?

Where is the dimension a god lives who will take Bird home?
I want to see it, I said to the Catalinas, to the Rincons,

to anyone listening in the dark. I said, Let me hear you
by any means: by horn, by fever, by night, even by some poem

attempting flight home.

The Bloodletting

It is the morning after
the morning after.
Your voice echoes like a broken
bottle muffled into my skin.
I won't let you do this
to myself, as for you,
you can always do
what you want.

                    Again.
How am I to stop you with
stark words, promises
glued together with blood,
or with the smell of love
a distant memory?
Will it drive in to save us
once more? Or will the smell
be dried and baked into ribbons
against a rusty knife?
I know it was meant in beauty,
but inside there are voices
urging me on to another distance
to a place that is even more
intimate than this one.
It, too, is a morning
made of blood, but it is sunlight
on a scarlet canyon wall in
early winter.
It does not scatter the heart
but gathers the branches tenderly
into a slender, dark woman.

Unmailed Letter

It's noon. I can hardly stand it.
If anything touches me, I am ashes.
Your laugh, and I considered myself
resurrected, but then made the correction
for time and space and it still added
to an irrational number.
It's elementary. You can't add
apples and oranges. I've mixed
faith with your distraction.
But I was never good at math.
Or with any test that meant jumping hoops
of water. This is how it is at specifically
noon. I am fire eaten by wind.
I drink water for a cure
that will teach me the fine art
of subtraction.

The Real Revolution Is Love,

I argue with Roberto on the slick-tiled patio
where houseplants as big as elms sway in a samba
breeze at four or five in the Managua morning
after too many Yerbabuenas and as many shots of
golden rum. And watch Pedro follow Diane up
her brown arm, over the shoulder of her cool dress,
the valleys of her neck to the place inside her
ear where he isn't speaking revolution. And Alonzo
tosses in the rhetoric made of too much rum and
the burden of being an American in a country
he no longer belongs to.

*What we are dealing with here are ideological
differences, political power,* he says to
impress a woman who is gorgeously intelligent
and who reminds me of the soft talc desert
of my lover's cheek. She doesn't believe
anything but the language of damp earth
beneath a banana tree at noon, and will soon
disappear in the screen of rum, with a man
who keeps his political secrets to himself
in favor of love.

I argue with Roberto, and laugh across the
continent to Diane, who is on the other side
of the flat, round table whose surface ships
would fall off if they sailed to the other
side. *We are Anishnabe and Creek. We have wars
of our own.* Knowing this we laugh and laugh,
until she disappears into the poinsettia forest
with Pedro, who is still arriving from Puerto Rico.

Palm trees flutter in smoldering tongues.
I can look through the houses, the wind, and hear
Jennifer's quick laughter become a train
that has no name. Columbus doesn't leave the
bow of the slippery ship, and Allen is standing at the rim
of Momotombo, looking into the blue, sad rain
of a boy's eyes. They will come back tomorrow.

*This is the land of revolution. You can do anything
you want,* Roberto tries to persuade me. I fight my way
through the cloud of rum and laughter, through the lines
of Spanish and spirits of the recently dead whose elbows
rustle the palm leaves. It is almost dawn and we are still
a long way from morning, but never far enough
to get away.

I do what I want, and take my revolution to bed with
me, alone. And awake in a story told by my ancestors
when they spoke a version of the very beginning,
of how so long ago we climbed the backbone of these
tortuous Americas. I listen to the splash of the Atlantic
and Pacific and see Columbus land once more,
over and over again.

This is not a foreign country, but the land of our dreams.

I listen to the gunfire we cannot hear, and begin
this journey with the light of knowing
the root of my own furious love.

Mad Love

And if I go
into the wild sweet of your eyes
will I know more
          of this burning country I love?

Deer Ghost

1.

I hear a deer outside; her glass voice of the invisible
calls my heart to stand up and weep in this fragile city.
The season changed once more, as if my childhood
was forced from me, stolen during the dream of the lion
fleeing the old-style houses my people used to make of mud
and straw to mother the source of burning. The skeleton
of stars encircling this misty world stares through the roof;
there is no hiding any more, and mystery is a skin that will never
quite fit. This is a night ghosts wander, and in this place
they are as nameless as the nightmare the muscles in my
left hand remember.

2.

I have failed once more and let the fire go out. I misunderstood
and left my world on your musk angel wings. Your fire scorched
my lips, but it was sweet, a bitter poetry. I can taste you
now as I squat on the earth floor of this home I abandoned
for you. On this street named for a warrior people, a street
named after bravery, I am lighting the fire that crawls from my spine
to the gods with a coal from my sister's flame. This is what names
me in the ways of my people, who have called me back.
The deer knows what it is doing wandering the streets of this
city; it has never forgotten the songs.

3.

I don't care what you say. The deer is no imaginary tale
I have created to fill this house because you left me.
There is more to this world than I have ever let on
to you, or anyone.

Song for the Deer and Myself
to Return On

This morning when I looked out the roof window
before dawn and a few stars were still caught
in the fragile weft of ebony night
I was overwhelmed. I sang the song Louis taught me:
a song to call the deer in Creek, when hunting,
and I am certainly hunting something as magic as deer
in this city far from the hammock of my mother's belly.
It works, of course, and deer came into this room
and wondered at finding themselves
in a house near downtown Denver.
Now the deer and I are trying to figure out a song
to get them back, to get all of us back,
because if it works I'm going with them.
And it's too early to call Louis
and nearly too late to go home.

(For Louis Oliver)

Javelina

The sun falls onto the bristly backs of foraging javelina west of the desert
oracle, and the soft streets stiffen with crawling dark. I drive South Tucson.
I am the one standing at a pay phone with a baby on her hip, just seventeen.
Do I need a job? Has the car broken down again? Does the license plate say
Oklahoma? I travel from a tribe whose name bears storm clouds, and have
entered a land where a drink of water is a way to pray. I was born of a blood
who wrestled the whites for freedom, and I have since lived dangerously in
a diminished system. I, too, still forage as the sun goes down: for lava
sustenance. The javelina know what I mean. I can no longer imagine this
poem without them, either their ghostly shapes of light-years reversed, or
the tracks now skating behind them in the sand.

I want to stop the car, and tell her she will find her way out of the soap
opera. *The mythic world will enter with the subtlety of a snake the color of
earth changing skin. Your wounded spirit is the chrysalis for a renascent
butterfly. Your son will graduate from high school. You have a daughter not
yet born, and you who thought you could say nothing, write poetry.*

And would she believe me?
And does she now?

Her husband comes out of the cheap room with more change and a Coke. I
cannot turn my head or lie; it has gotten me nowhere. I leave her there. But
for years I pray for rain, for her beaten spirit to lift up and rain and rain.
The cicadas enter with a song at the torn edge; they call forth the burning
sunset the color of the lips of the unseen guardian of mist. A renegade turtle
hides beneath damp runners of a plant with red berries; tastes rain. I
imagine the talk of pigs and hear them speak the coolest promise of spiny
leaves. Their prevalent nightmare has entered recent genetic memory, as the
smell of gunpowder mixed with human sweat.

I have done time on their streets, said an elder with thick tusks of wisdom.
*And I have understood this desert without them. It is sweeter than the
blooms of prickly pear. It is sweeter than rain.*

Rainy Dawn

I can still close my eyes and open them four floors up looking south and west from the hospital, the approximate direction of Acoma, and farther on to the roofs of the houses of the gods who have learned there are no endings, only beginnings. That day so hot, heat danced in waves off bright car tops, we both stood poised at that door from the east, listened for a long time to the sound of our grandmothers' voices, the brushing wind of sacred wings, the rattle of raindrops in dry gourds. I had to participate in the dreaming of you into memory, cupped your head in the bowl of my body as ancestors lined up to give you a name made of their dreams cast once more into this stew of precious spirit and flesh. And let you go, as I am letting you go once more in this ceremony of the living, thirteen years later. And when you were born I held you wet and unfolding, like a butterfly newly born from the chrysalis of my body. And breathed with you as you breathed your first breath. Then was your promise to take it on like the rest of us, this immense journey, for love, for rain.

Crystal Lake

I caught crawdads and let them go. Baited hooks with my grandfather, watched iridescent dragonflies fly between heaven and hell. I was restless in adolescent heat, wandered the rocky banks of Crystal Lake. No one else there: too hot, too humid, except for the cool lake of the fish, water moccasins slicing through the invisible current, a turtle's nose above water, and my grandfather pulling another bass out of the underworld. I watch it flip and leap in the cutting air. The gills bleeding this gift of air onto the gritty rocks. I say stop this suffering, but my mouth evokes nothing in the flat, wet blanket of noon. I am too curious of my own death, riding the sling between my newborn hips, to pay respect or help. We take the boat back through the finger of the lake. Caves echo each paddle stroke, suck the ripple in and turn them into our own voices calling to us from blind halls. Come home, come home, the meaning feeding the crumbling guilt at the sudden turn of my body. Bats fly at perfect random from the limestone cliffs, follow the invisible moon. I don't remember any words, but the shushing of the sun through dried grass, nibble of carp at the bottom of the boat, the slow melting of my body. My grandfather towed us through the lake. We skimmed over mythical fish he once caught, over fish who were as long as rainbows after the coming storm.

A Hard Rain

I awaken to a sky with no sun
  only clouds carrying rain
                    to China
    not meant for here
              but I am soaked, will not ripen.
It's not a seed that causes children
    to bloom, or others to be sucked out
                    by a sterile whirlwind.
      It's not blood or some strange moon
            whistling hard overhead.
Fertility is the heart
                signaled by the smell of yellow paint
      stroked across a circle
      by a sound
                    that forces me up out of silent nights.
It is a raw and wild taste that poises
      at the end of my tongue
                    then dissolves.
          Until I awaken again to swollen clouds
    and your dark hand on my thigh
              the only hot sun I want to feel.

Summer Night

The moon is nearly full,
                the humid air sweet like melon.
Flowers that have cupped the sun all day
                        dream of iridescent wings
under the long dark sleep.
                Children's invisible voices call out
in the glimmering moonlight.
                   Their parents play worn-out records
of the cumbia. Behind the screen door
                    their soft laughter swells
into the rhythm of a smooth guitar.
                 I watch the world shimmer
inside this globe of a summer night,
                  listen to the wobble of her
spin and dive. It happens all the time, waiting for you
                      to come home.
There is an ache that begins
                in the sound of an old blues song.
It becomes a house where all the lights have gone out
                    but one.
And it burns and burns
                until there is only the blue smoke of dawn
and everyone is sleeping in someone's arms
                    even the flowers
even the sound of a thousand silences.
                And the arms of night
in the arms of day.
           Everyone except me.
But then the smell of damp honeysuckle twisted on the vine.
And the turn of the shoulder
                of the ordinary spirit who keeps watch
over this ordinary street.
           And there you are, the secret
of your own flower of light
                blooming in the miraculous dark.

Bleed Through

I don't believe in promises, but there you are,
balancing on a tightrope of sound.

                You sneak into the world
inside a labyrinth of flame,

          break the walls beneath my ribs.
I yearn to sing; a certain note can spiral stars,

        or knock the balance of the world askew.
Inside your horn lives a secret woman

           who says she knows the power of the womb,
can transform massacres into gold, her own heartache

          into a ruby stone.
Her anger is yours and when her teeth bite through

              a string of glass
you awaken, and it is not another dream

          but your arms around a woman
       who was once a dagger between your legs.
There are always ways to fall asleep,

         but to be alive is to forsake

             the fear of blood.
And dreams aren't excuses anymore. You are not behind a smoking mirror,
but inside a ceremony of boulders that has survived

           your many deaths.
It is not by accident you watch the sun

         become your heart
     sink into your belly then reappear in a town

          that magnetically attracts you.
What attracts cannot naturally be separated.
    A black hole reversed is a white-hot star,

             unravels this night
inside a song that is the same wailing cry as blue.
   There are no words, only sounds

          that lead us into the darkest nights,
where stars burn into ice

      where the dead arise again

         to walk in shoes of fire.

Blue Elliptic

All the lights in the house are burning.
In the other room Zinger still wheezes,
then puts her raggy head between her paws
and sleeps. She leaps but it is not
real. Already she anticipates your return,
hears the van pulling up, cracking the
iced asphalt, the rattle of equipment, and
your lullaby voice soothing her ear. All
her nerves run on that sound. And in the
other room the fish swim musically in their
watery cage. Their sense of concave horizon
points to a foreign sky. The heater shakes
and blows from the basement, and outside
someone loses his voice, calling to an angel
he has never seen before. And all I can
remember to tell you is the talk of a meteor
shower. To drive to it is impossible in
this weather, but close by are velvet deer
stalking the moon on the shaggy ice. And
closer still you are in Vail playing the
gorgeous blues with Maxine and the crazy
quartet. The Geminids are falling falling
from one sky to another, onto the antlers
of the luminescent deer, onto the roof
of this house, and did you see
as your fingers climbed your tenor for
the smell of a flower that would never
prosper in this world, did you see

as you made that frightening leap
through the diminished world
into the lapis asylum

did you see

Healing Animal

On this day when you have needed to sleep forever,
to forgive the pained animal kneading

                          your throat,
Sleep, your back curled against my belly.
I will make you something to drink,

                              from a cup of frothy stars
from the *somewhere there is the perfect sound*
called up from the best-told stories

                        of benevolent gods,
who have nothing better to do.

                     And I ask you
what bitter words are ruining your soft-skinned village,
because I want to make a poem that will cup

                 the inside of your throat
like the fire in the palm of a healing animal. Like
the way Coltrane knew love in the fluid shape
of a saxophone

             that could change into the wings of a blue angel.
He tasted the bittersweet roots of this crazy world,
and spit them out into the center of our musical

                 jazzed globe.
Josiah's uncle brought his music

     to the Papago center of the world

            and music climbed out of his trombone
into the collected heartbeat of his tribe.
They had never heard anything like it,

        but it was the way they had remembered, the way
"Chief" Joe Moore must have known when he sang

           for the very first time
through the brass-boned monster.
All through the last few nights I have watched you fight for yourself
with the eyes I was warned against opening.

        You think you are asleep
when you turn off the lights, and we blend into the same

          hot-skinned sky.

The land called miracle is the daughter you never died for and she
stands at the edge of the bed with her slim hand
                                        against your cheek.
Your music is a crystal wall with a thousand mouths, kin to trains and
sounds that haven't yet been invented,
                                        and you walk back and forth
through it to know it won't betray you.
And in the last seconds before the breaking light,
when you are nearly broken with the secret antelope
of compassion,
                        when the last guardian angel has flown west to the Pacific
to see someone else through their nightly death,
a homefire is slowly kindled in the village of your body.
And the smoke of dawn turns all your worded enemies
into ashes that will never rise.
Mythic cattle graze in your throat, washing it with milk.
And you will sing forever.

(For L. N. and Michael Harper)

Rainy Night

What she must have felt
those solid crusted
heart rises
against the eastern edge
of her own life
going down
        once more
into blue midnight
her patent-leather shoes
muddy and stained
love
    at the end of the train line
Billie
    you come home now
we would hold you closer than
the pain
you felt you deserved
need you
      like the last train
to leave New York City
in the rain

(For Billie Holiday)

City of Fire

Here is a city built of passion
where live many houses
with never falling night
in many rooms.
Through this entrance cold
is no longer a thief,
and in this place your heart
will never be a murderer.
Come, sweet,
I am a house with many rooms.
There is no end.
Each room is a street to the next world.
Where live other cities beneath
incendiary skies. And you have made
a fire in every room.
Come.
Lie with me before the flame.
I will dream you a wolf
and suckle you newborn.
I will dream you a hawk
and circle this city in your
racing heart.
I will dream you the wind,
taste salt air on my lips until
I take you apart raw.
Come here.

We will make a river,
flood this city built of passion
with fire,
with a revolutionary fire.

Santa Fe

The wind blows lilacs out of the east. And it isn't lilac season. And I am walking the street in front of St. Francis Cathedral in Santa Fe. Oh, and it's a few years earlier and more. That's how you tell real time. It is here, it is there. The lilacs have taken over everything: the sky, the narrow streets, my shoulders, my lips. I talk lilac. And there is nothing else until a woman the size of a fox breaks through the bushes, breaks the purple web. She is tall and black and gorgeous. She is the size of a fox on the arm of a white man who looks and tastes like cocaine. She lies for cocaine, dangles on the arm of cocaine. And lies to me now from a room in the DeVargas Hotel, where she has eaten her lover, white powder on her lips. That is true now; it is not true anymore. Eventually space curves, walks over and taps me on the shoulder. On the sidewalk I stand near St. Francis; he has been bronzed, a perpetual tan, with birds on his hand, his shoulder, deer at his feet. I am Indian and in this town I will never be a saint. I am seventeen and shy and wild. I have been up until three at a party, but there is no woman in the DeVargas Hotel, for that story hasn't yet been invented. A man whose face I will never remember, and never did, drives up on a Harley-Davidson. There are lilacs on his arm; they spill out from the spokes of his wheels. He wants me on his arm, on the back of his lilac bike touring the flower kingdom of San Francisco. And for a piece of time the size of a nickel, I think, maybe. But maybe is vapor, has no anchor here in the sun beneath St. Francis Cathedral. And space is as solid as the bronze statue of St. Francis, the fox breaking through the lilacs, my invention of this story, the wind blowing.

Climbing the Streets of
Worcester, Mass.

Houses lean forward with their hands
on thin hips.
   I walk past their eyes
of pigeon grey, hear someone
playing horn, and there's the wind
trying to teach some trees
     to fly.
It could happen.
    LA is tempted by the ocean.
And sleeping storms erupt the weakest hearts.
I scan the street. Know up one hill
groans a sacred fire
    and down the next
could be a crazy trick:
     three crows laugh
kick up the neighbor's trash.
Telling jokes
   they re-create the world.
All night
   while I was making other plans
the wind drew circles around this town;
scraped clean the dead skin
     of its soul
but left three crows, a horn
some trees
   to talk it back again.

A Winning Hand

In this university town of winners, the wind is a blur through the dandelions and nurtured grass on the lawn outside my office, and you are here, but have gone on to the buffalo-skinned dream that has fallen in the cracks between the small towns that make a necklace from Medicine Lake to Missoula. Indians still dry jerky in the risky wind, test the water for visions of buffalo, who were more than just meat sustenance. Aren't our bodies mostly wind? And are cursed, like the rest of us, with being able to smell but not see the world we are crazy for. You knew that place, traveled it until it drove you crazy, too, to think like one of the beautiful native misfits. In Albuquerque in either seventy-eight or nine you stunned my students from Indian School into returning to the ghost towns their memories had become, in that auditorium built in a town spit into existence by dry-lipped conquistadores who wanted only gold and Indian wives. Someone must have prophesied what they feared. Nez couldn't take it, turned wads of clay into glossy bowls, but they still weren't enough to hold her words. She abandoned us in that auditorium for the corner bar of the lost poets. After your last poem, your heart tearing us apart, we all left to find her, and had to chase ourselves out of that place. There was only the magnetism of ghosts driving us back, into the winning hand.

I don't think I looked back, or believed you had ever gone. When I hit the Montana border last spring during the last hard storm, the wind nearly knocked me over. And it wasn't poetry I heard, but something like the moan and laughter of a player with the best hand, a touch of luck.

This time it's all or nothing, and there won't be any more losers in this field of tens and one-eyed jacks.

(For Richard Hugo)

Day of the Dead

This is a witching season, the pivotal mouth as the world of the dead, staggered with the living, opens. Children dressed as spirits and monsters suck candy, parade the streets. Wind is electric, sharp as truth. Spirits play crack-the-whip in the abyss. I have needed to talk but you are insanely absent and I have become insanely mute. When I hold the compass you gave me, the needle points in a direction that is neither yes nor no. The star map has become symbols I can't describe because it delineates a system entering a distant compassionate universe. I have built a fire in the cave of my body, and hope the devil wind gives it a chance. There is an underground river with blind fish nearby. What do they choose in this season where there must be spirit fish with wings? I cannot sing song of either staying or leaving unless I know what shape it takes when it leaves my mouth. And which direction, because I forgot to tell you that love changes molecular structure. I am transformed but without a map. The Day of the Dead marks skeletal transition and flowers bloom in the snow. I have checked the weather, and will tend the fire until I am forced to join the parade. Then I will be a madman. I will drink whiskey and slow-dance with slim boys, rock with glitter angels, before going home alone. Tomorrow I will feed the dead. Then I must find you.

Crossing Water

I return like a detective to the dance floor in New York, or was it someplace
else invented to look like October? I turn back to a music the d.j. never
played because the room was too blue for falling angels. Nothing by Aretha,
nothing by chance. A woman chased by spirits kept asking you to dance,
made a gift of her hands. I add her to the evidence: we were there. She was
a witness but I don't have her name. Or yours or mine, or was the shift in
axis an event in the imagination? I should be writing poems to change the
world. They would appear as a sacrifice of deer for the starving. Or poems
of difficulty to place my name in the Book of Poets. I should get on with it.
Instead I walk back through the dark in my shoes the color of hearts to find
us embraced in a ring of smoke. Hey, I wanted you in your jeans and casual
sweater with your caramel lips. The next time I looked we were laughing
and drunk, kissing in the car before crossing water. The Brooklyn Bridge
tilted to heaven. I want you eternally ever, but this is the puzzle. There is
no dance floor on Nineteenth Street. The woman with spirits left no
forwarding address. There is no getaway car, no Brooklyn Bridge. The
evidence floats by like rings over sweet water. Like rings over sweet
water.

Original Memory

When Rabbit doubted the miracle of creation at the beginning of the world (for Rabbit was surely there, balancing on the not-yet abyss of past and future), doubt sprang from his heart and humans were created. What does love have to do with this, except it's early on some morning that will pass as fast as the earth spins at 18.5 miles per second, or quicker if one is making love with someone desired and forbidden, or slower if one is being tortured by someone who claims to do it out of love, love for the state, the state of political affairs, which, too, somehow must begin in the heart (but here is a heart betrayed by childhood catastrophe, or tormented by original memory, memory as old as Rabbit's heart cracking open because he couldn't believe in the perfection of newborn sea perch, or the yawning of the first corn sprout, and let loose doubt into the world in the shape of humans). It could be any day on the scale of earthly days, which of course varies according to belief. When I am inside the Muscogee world, which is not a flip side of the Western time chain but a form of music staggered in the ongoing event of earth calisthenics, the past and the future are the same tug-of-war. Love is always love but we're convinced there isn't enough there either, so we pull ourselves out of our ceremonial spiral of prayer, understood relationship, into this other world because whatever world we are entering or leaving we are still looking for love. But Western time is a dominant white man, perhaps Doubt himself, who demands of the world utmost respect and servitude, worships invention and calls it love. But that's not what moves me this early morning on a day that is a repetition, a variation on a theme of others, a day born of careful urge to proclaim itself in the world, an event that has perhaps created us, so that we may participate with it, a day in which I am created, yearning for perfection of love. Last night, I played saxophone duets with a friend. This was not in the Muscogee world (though as elements interplay throughout the evening, I am never far away). We are both heartbroken, mourning lovers who disappeared some time ago into old calendar pages. But the events are perfected as we make music, and here is Doubt again, making ready for another leap into the world, to re-create itself again. Doubt here isn't a white man, but beautiful lovers who left in the same way a day turns on the heels of sunset to go on to some other world of its creation. In the Muscogee world, one would have a circle of relatives (everyone is ulti-

Rabbit is a trickster in Muscogee (Creek) mythology.

mately a relative) recalling similar events, to establish connection, and to convey the event lovingly into a past. (But how do we know it doesn't re-create a similar event, again?) In the world of the jammed city I am flying on a saxophone with someone who is not my lover, trying to leap past 4/4 time to understand it. Was it love? Or are all events imaginary? In this world the turn of events is praised by love songs: either Bobby Caldwell sweetly with "What You Won't Do for Love," or a pale madonna skipping on the vanishing stage of your love. And that is the ceremony. We sip wine, do a hit of courage, each of us imagining another spin of the wheel, and take up our horns again. Rabbit, who invented the saxophone and who must have invented our imaginary lovers, laughs through millennia. And who are we to make sense of this slit of impossible time?

If I Think About You Again It Will Be the Fifty-third Monday of Next Year

A musical animal like Weather Report blows through the black market on
this snowy Monday and I can go anywhere I want. So why does this sound
lead to the face of the only one I could have hated. Hatred is a vice that
smells like four mutilated cats smoking in a gasoline fire. And worse. And
here I am stirring an imagination that has always got me into trouble,
thinking what I could do to you. It wouldn't be pretty as the dusk sun
slipping from one bed to the next. Or feel like a sultry fish on the dance
floor with a woman you have loved forever. Nothing like that is what I
would do to you. I could make you the fifth cat and turn my back. I could say
your name backward and send it to a warring star. Or, better yet, erase it,
your whole story a sterile page, and I would rewrite it without you in it. Yes.
Let me begin with a day like this, a musical animal like Weather Report
blowing through the black market on this snowy snowy Monday and I can go
anywhere I want, and do
without you.

Nine Lives

A storm tangles in the east and will disappear in a paradise of midnight. The moon is a stripped lizard half here and half visible by the eye on the other side of the world. Someone up the alley is singing Happy Birthday to a packed house. I am downwind of the beer foam, the laughter. Death with its coat of tender wings is close to my shoulder, while the neighbor's cat fights for one of its nine lives. In the morning the winner will be grinning at the door of my sleep. I know you can understand the structure of the spiraled world in an ordinary moment, or by falling through the crack of a perfumed nightmare. Cicadas climb out of the carcasses their voices make, into their wings of fragile promises to glide over the wet grass. We are all spun within a crescendo of abalone light, unseen beneath the wild storm. What spins us now, in this neighborhood chrysalis at exactly midnight? Don't tell me unless it will turn me into something as perfect as a perfect monarch butterfly.

We Encounter Nat King Cole as We
Invent the Future

Camme and I listened to Nat King Cole and she sweetly lay her head
on the shoulder of some well-slicked man and off
she went some slow easy step some thirty years ago; it wasn't
yesterday but ghosts of time in tilted hats are ushered
by our heartbeats into the living room as we eat fried chicken,
drink Cokes and talk about swing, don't talk
about heartbreak but it's in the stirred air. How we loved,
and how we love. There is no end to it.
One song can be a crack-the-whip snapping everything
we were in the lifetime of a song back
into the tempest of dreams. And when the Cokes are gone,
chicken bones drying in the sun,
radio shifted into another plane of time, I don't know
what to believe. My heart's a steady tattoo of roses.
Camme and I go to sleep in our different houses, she without
her dancing man, and me with my imaginary lover
outlined in smoke, coming up the road. There's a song
that hasn't been written yet; the first notes
are a trio of muses in a songwriter's ear. That song will invent
my lover of evening light, of musky genius,
I know it. As sure as I know Nat King Cole wore white suede
shoes, and smelled like spice hair cream,
as sure as the monsoon rains come praising the dry Sonoran.
Yesterday I turned north on Greasewood
the long way home and was shocked to see a double rainbow
two-stepping across the valley. Suddenly
there were twin gods bending over to plant something like
themselves in the wet earth, a song
larger than all our cheap hopes, our small-town radios,
whipping everything back
into the geometry of dreams: became Nat King Cole
became the sultry blue moon became all
perfumed romantic strangers became Camme and me
became love
suddenly

Desire

Say I chew desire and water is an explosion
of sugar wings in my mouth.

Say it tastes of you.

Say I could drown because you left
for the time it takes a blackbird to understand
a pine tree.

Say we enter the pine woods at dawn.

We never slept and the only opium we smoked
was what became of our mingled breath.

Say the stars have never learned
to say good-bye. (One is a jewel
of blue magic in your perfect ear.)

Say all of this is true and more

than there are blackbirds
in a heaven of blackbirds.

(For J.)

Hieroglyphic

June, I don't have to use magic burned into roots of antelope words
to tell you what I mean when I say I met myself in the Egyptian Room

just a few days before my thirty-sixth birthday. It wasn't vertigo, though
vertigo is common in the bowels of the concrete monster. Crossing Fifth

Avenue was a trick of the imagination. It wasn't that. By the time I had
forgiven the stolen pyramidal gateway my heart had become a phoenix of

swallowed myths. They appeared as angry angels stalking the streets, who
prophesy resurrection of flowers as they tether skeleton horses, stake out

the warmest corners. I have seen them write poetry in your poetry. They'll
tell you there is no heaven or hell; it's all the same.

I have seen heaven in a woman's eyes the color of burnt almonds.
I have seen hell in those same eyes, and I have jumped.
It's all the same.

I entered that room naked except for the dream of carrying a water jar to
the river. And within that dream a crocodile cruised the grasses, watched

me dip it, then drove me down. I remembered none of it as the spin of
broken sky replaced my meager human memory. And woke up, five

years old in a sweaty army blanket on a cot in Oklahoma, to see the false
fronts of sepulchers painted with the masks of rulers, the soul

underlined with kohl, my child's eyelash a leap in time. I once again
offered my rebel spirit up to the living. And awoke, startled to cradle

my ribs of water years later in an Egyptian Room that is merely fractile of
Egypt, to take on this torture of language to describe once more what can't

be born on paper. It goes something like this: When the mythic spiral of time turned its beaded head and understood what was going on, it snapped. All

these years I had been sleeping in the mind of the snake, June. I have to tell this to someone.

(For June Jordan)

54

The Book of Myths

When I entered the book of myths
                      in your sandalwood room on the granite island,
   I did not ask for a way out.
This is not the century for false pregnancy
                 in these times when myths
                       have taken to the streets.
There is no more imagination; we are in it now, girl.
   We traveled the stolen island of Manhattan
           in a tongue of wind off the Atlantic
      shaking our shells, in our mad skins.
I did not tell you when I saw Rabbit sobbing and laughing
                  as he shook his dangerous bag of tricks
     into the mutiny world on that street outside Hunter.
Out came you and I blinking our eyes once more, entwined in our loves
    and hates as we set off to recognize the sweet
and bitter gods who walk beside us, whisper madness
in our invisible ears any ordinary day.
   I have fallen in love a thousand times over; every day is a common
miracle of salt roses, of fire in the prophecy wind, and now and then
            I taste the newborn blood in my daughter's
              silk hair, as if she were not nearly a woman
    brown and electric in her nearly womanly self.
There is a Helen in every language; in American her name is Marilyn
              but in my subversive country,
    she is dark earth and round and full of names
dressed in bodies of women
    who enter and leave the knife wounds of this terrifyingly
beautiful land;
            we call ourselves ripe, and pine tree, and woman.
    In the book of myths that fell open in your room of unicorns
I did not imagine the fiery goddess in the middle of the island.
She is a sweet trick of flame,

had everyone dancing, laughing and telling the stories
that unglue the talking spirit from the pages.
When the dawn light came on through the windows,
          I understood how my bones would one day
       stand up, brush off the lovely skin like a satin blouse
and dance with foolish grace to heaven.

Death Is a Woman

I walk these night hours between the dead and the living, and see you
two-step with Death as if nothing ever ended.
We buried you in Okmulgee, on a day when leaves already buried
the earth in scarlet and crisp ochre.
Four years isn't long on this spiral of tangential stories.
I can already see my own death trying on my shoes
as clearly as I saw your young demise in the early fifties
as she tripped the street before you in high heels.
I smelled her sweet perfume like a carnival in my childhood
and knew even then you would never be satisfied
until you had her.
Tonight I see the tracks the sun makes at the fold of unreason,
a space where geese disappear like teeth behind the lips
of night.
                    I am ready to run.
Instead I'll make up another story about who I think you really were
with the words left in the mouth of a cardinal
who startled us your last summer.
Six months later you flew from the sour trailer that dissolved
from metal to salt air, into her arms.
I see you dip and sway on the mythical dance floor
just the other side of this room of whirling atoms, my father
of Tiger people, who drank whiskey thrown back with bleached women
all of them blonde except for my Cherokee mother and the Pottowatamie
who once when you were dying gambled your money as you drove yourself
spitting blood to the hospital.
I have a photograph of you with my mother, from before
or after I was born.
Here you sit in Cain's Ballroom, reeking of Lucky Strikes
your hair slick and black as a beaver's, feeling better
than you could ever believe.
And my mother on the same side as your heart
looking past the camera, into her imagined future without you,
fiercely into the brutal eyes of the woman who seduced you
and won.

You are dancing with Death now, you were dancing with her then.
And there is nothing I could ever do about it.
Not then, or now.
I have nothing to prove your fierce life, except paper
that turns back to dust.
Except this song that plays over and over
that you keep dancing to.

Transformations

This poem is a letter to tell you that I have smelled the hatred you have tried to find me with; you would like to destroy me. Bone splintered in the eye of one you choose to name your enemy won't make it better for you to see. It could take a thousand years if you name it that way, but then, to see after all that time, never could anything be so clear. Memory has many forms. When I think of early winter I think of a blackbird laughing in the frozen air; guards a piece of light. (I saw the whole world caught in that sound, the sun stopped for a moment because of tough belief.) I don't know what that has to do with what I am trying to tell you except that I know you can turn a poem into something else. This poem could be a bear treading the far northern tundra, smelling the air for sweet alive meat. Or a piece of seaweed stumbling in the sea. Or a blackbird, laughing. What I mean is that hatred can be turned into something else, if you have the right words, the right meanings, buried in that tender place in your heart where the most precious animals live. Down the street an ambulance has come to rescue an old man who is slowly losing his life. Not many can see that he is already becoming the backyard tree he has tended for years, before he moves on. He is not sad, but compassionate for the fears moving around him.

That's what I mean to tell you. On the other side of the place you live stands
a dark woman. She has been trying to talk to you for years.
You have called the same name in the middle of a nightmare,
from the center of miracles. She is beautiful.
This is your hatred back. She loves you.

Nine Below

Across the frozen Bering Sea is the invisible border
of two warring countries. I am loyal to neither,

only to the birds who fly over, laugh at the ridiculous
ways of humans, know wars destroy dreams, divide the

country inside us. Last night there was a breaking
wave, in the center of a dream war. You were there, but

I couldn't see you. Woke up cold in a hot house. Didn't
sleep but fought the distances I had imagined, and went

back to find you. I called my heart's dogs, gave them
the sound of your blue saxophone to know you by, and let

them smell the shirt you wore when we last made love.
I walked with them along the white sea, and

crossed to the fiery plain of my dreaming. We circled
the place; you weren't there. I found nothing I could see,

no trace of war, of you, but the dogs barked, rolled
in your smell, ears pricked at what they could hear that

I couldn't. They ran to me, licked the smell of the wet
tracks of your mouth from my neck, my shoulder. They

smelled your come on my fingers, my face. They felt the
quivering nerve of emotion that forced me to live. It

made them nervous, excited. I loosened my mind's rein;
let them find you.

I watched them follow the invisible connection. They
traveled a spiral arc through an Asiatic burst of time.

There were no false boundaries between countries, between
us. They climbed the polar ice, saw it melt.

They flew through the shimmering houses of the gods,
crossed over into your childhood, and then south.

When they arrived in your heart's atmosphere it was
an easy sixty degrees. The war was over; it had never

begun. And you were alive and laughing, standing beneath
a fat sun, calling me home.

Heartshed

You dream a heated chase.
Your heart pumps time through you
                              into lakes of fire
and I can't sleep at night
because you have found me.

You keep coming back, the one who knows
the sound they call
                    "in the beginning."
It doesn't mean going backward.
Our bones are built of spirals.
The sun
        circling.
                  Ravens hang the walls
calling memory.
You could call it a war; it has been before.

I have killed you many times in jealousy,
beat you while you dreamed in the arms
of another lover.
                  You shot me down in a war
that was only our own,
                      my brother, my sister.
The names could be all that truly changes,
                              not love.

I walk into another room inside
                          your skin house.
I open your legs with my tongue.
The war is not over but inside you
                          the night is hot
and my fingers walk their way up your spine.
Your spirit rattles in your bones and yes
let's dance this all again
                  another beginning.

Memory is triggered
                by polished stones spit up
        from the center of the earth,
by ashy rock that crumbles in your hand.
Some are unborn children, others old ones
                who chose to learn patience, to know currents.

You dream a solid red cliff. The sun rises again
over the eastern horizon. Saturn spins
in her rings.
                The names change.
                                Ravens call.
Lean up against me full with the words that have
kept you silent. Lean with the silence
                                that imagines you.
I forgive you, forgive myself
from the beginning
                this heartshed.

(For L. D.)

Eagle Poem

To pray you open your whole self
To sky, to earth, to sun, to moon
To one whole voice that is you.
And know there is more
That you can't see, can't hear,
Can't know except in moments
Steadily growing, and in languages
That aren't always sound but other
Circles of motion.
Like eagle that Sunday morning
Over Salt River. Circled in blue sky
In wind, swept our hearts clean
With sacred wings.
We see you, see ourselves and know
That we must take the utmost care
And kindness in all things.
Breathe in, knowing we are made of
All this, and breathe, knowing
We are truly blessed because we
Were born, and die soon within a
True circle of motion,
Like eagle rounding out the morning
Inside us.
We pray that it will be done
In beauty.
In beauty.

About the Author

Joy Harjo was born in Tulsa, Oklahoma, in 1951. Her books of poetry include *The Woman Who Fell From the Sky* (W.W. Norton, 1994), which received the Oklahoma Book Arts Award; *Secrets from the Center of the World* (1989); *She Had Some Horses* (1983); and *What Moon Drove Me to This?* (1979). She also performs her poetry and plays saxophone with her band, Poetic Justice. Her many honors include The American Indian Distinguished Achievement in the Arts Award, the Josephine Miles Poetry Award, the Mountains and Plains Booksellers Award, the William Carlos Williams Award, and fellowships from the Arizona Commission on the Arts, the Witter Bynner Foundation, and the National Endowment for the Arts.

About the Artist

Jaune Quick-to-See Smith is a member of the Flathead tribe, Montana. She is a painter who exhibits internationally and is an activist/spokeswoman for both traditional and contemporary Native artists. She has founded two cooperatives: the Coup Marks on the Flathead Reserve and the Grey Canyon Artists in Albuquerque.

About the Book

This book was composed on the Mergenthaler 202 in Trump Medieval, a contemporary typeface based on classical prototypes. It was designed by the German graphic artist and type designer Georg Trump (1895–1986). It was initially issued in 1954, in the form of foundry type and linecasting matrices, by C. E. Weber Typefoundry of Stuttgart. The book was composed by Graphic Composition of Athens, Georgia, and designed and produced by Kachergis Book Design, Pittsboro, North Carolina.